CSU Poetry Series XXXVIII

Tim Seibles

Hurdy-Gurdy

Cleveland State University Poetry Center

ACKNOWLEDGMENTS

Some of the poems in this collection have appeared in the following periodicals.

BLACK AMERICAN LITERATURE FORUM: "For Brothers Everywhere" (under the title "The Shit Didn Hit Nuttin But Net")
CALLALOO: "Like This"
CALLIOPE: "The Debt," "Dogs," "You Damn Right"
CIMARRON REVIEW: "Trying For Fire"
INDIANA REVIEW: "Natasha In A Mellow Mood," "Slow Dance"
KENYON REVIEW: "After All," "What It Comes Down To"
MISSISSIPPI REVIEW: "Boris By Candlelight"
PASSAGES NORTH: "Each Letter," "Sweet Onion Soup"
POETRY MISCELLANY: "Shape"
SPOON RIVER QUARTERLY: "Appetite," "The Good City," "The Lamps," "The Motion"
SULPHUR RIVER: "A Jitterbug For Spring," "Notes," "Rain"
TAOS REVIEW: "Treatise"

I would like to thank the National Endowment for the Arts and Provincetown Fine Arts Work Center for the fellowships which allowed me the time to complete several of the poems in this collection.

I am also grateful to the following authors and teachers whose vision and inspiration helped to bring these poems into being: Jack Myers, Mark Cox, Rick Jackson, Susan Mitchell, Paul Laurence Dunbar, Margaret Walker, Pablo Neruda, Cesar Vallejo, Ai, Franz Wright, Cornelius Eady, Sharon Olds, and Stephen Dobyns.

ISBN 0-914946-98-6

Library of Congress Catalog Card Number: 92-70729

Funded Through
Ohio Arts Council

727 East Main Street
Columbus, Ohio 43205-1796
(614) 466-2613

CONTENTS

I. Meep

II. Appetite

III. Rain

Nothing perishes, it is merely lost till a surgeon's electrode starts the music of an old player piano whose scrolls are dust. Or you yourself do it, tossing in the restless nights, or even in the day on a strange street when a hurdy-gurdy plays. Nothing is lost, but it can never be again as it was. You will only find the bits and cry out because they were yourself.

—Loren Eiseley

I. Meep

TRYING FOR FIRE

Right now, even if a muscular woman wanted
to teach me the power of her skin
I'd probably just stand here with my hands
jammed in my pockets. Tonight
I'm feeling weak as water, watching the wind
bandage the moon. That's how it is tonight:
sky like tar, thin gauzy clouds,
a couple lame stars. A car rips by—
the driver's cigarette pinwheels past
the dog I saw hit this afternoon.
One second he was trotting along
with his wet nose tasting the air,
next thing I know he's off the curb,
a car swerves and, bam, it's over. For an instant,
he didn't seem to understand he was dying—
he lifted his head as if he might still reach
the dark-green trash bags half-open
on the other side of the street.

I wish someone could tell me
how to live in the city. My friends
just shake their heads and shrug. I
can't go to church—I'm embarrassed by things
preachers say we should believe.
I would talk to my wife, but she's worried
about the house. Whenever she listens
she hears the shingles giving in
to the rain. If I read the paper
I start believing some stranger
has got my name in his pocket—
on a matchbook next to his knife.

When I was twelve I'd take out the trash—
the garage would open like some ogre's cave
while just above my head the Monday Night Movie

stepped out of the television, and my parents
leaned back in their chairs. I can still hear
my father's voice coming through the floor,
"Boy, make sure you don't make a mess down there."
I remember the red-brick caterpillar of row houses
on Belfield Avenue and, not much higher than the rooftops,
the moon, soft and pale as a nun's thigh.

I had a plan back then—my feet were made
for football: each toe had the heart
of a different animal, so I ran
ten ways at once. I knew I'd play pro
and live with my best friend, and
when Vanessa let us pull up her sweater
those deep-brown balloony mounds made me believe
in a world where eventually you could touch
whatever you didn't understand.

If I was afraid of anything it was
my bedroom when my parents made me
turn out the light: that knocking noise
that kept coming from the walls,
the shadow shapes by the bookshelf,
the feeling that something was always there
just waiting for me to close my eyes.
But only sleep would get me, and I'd
wake up running for my bike, my life
jingling like a little bell on the breeze.
I understood so little that I
understood it all, and I still know
what it meant to be one of the boys
who had never kissed a girl.

I never did play pro football.
I never got to do my mad-horse,
mountain goat, happy-wolf dance
for the blaring fans in the Astro Dome.
I never snagged a one-hander over the middle

against Green Bay and stole my snaky way
down the sideline for the game-breaking six.

And now, the city is crouched like a mugger
behind me—right outside, in the alley behind my door,
a man stabbed this guy for his wallet, and sometimes
I see this four-year-old with his face all bruised,
his father holding his hand like a vise. When I
turn on the radio the music is just like the news.
So, what should I do—close my eyes and hope
whatever's out there will just let me sleep?
I won't sleep tonight. I'll stay near my TV
and watch the police get everybody.

Across the street a woman is letting
her phone ring. I see her in the kitchen
stirring something on the stove. Farther off
a small dog chips the quiet with his bark.
Above me the moon looks like a nickel
in a murky little creek. This
is the same moon that saw me twelve,
without a single bill to pay, zinging
soup can tops into the dark—I called them
flying saucers. This is the same
white light that touched dinosaurs, that
found the first people trying for fire.

It must have been very good, that moment
when wood smoke turned to flickering, when
they believed night was broken
once and for all—I wonder what almost-words
were spoken. I wonder how long
before that first flame went out.

FOR BROTHERS EVERYWHERE

There is a schoolyard that runs
from here to the dark's fence
where brothers keep goin to the hoop, keep
risin up with baske'balls ripe as pumpkins
toward rims hung like piñatas, pinned
like thunderclouds to the sky's wide chest
an'everybody is spinnin an' bankin
off the glass, finger-rollin off the glass
with the same soft touch you'd give
the head of a child, *a chile witta*
big-ass pumpkin head, who stands
in the schoolyard lit by brothers—postin up,
givin, goin, taking the lane, flashin off
the pivot, dealin behind the back, between
the legs, cockin the rock an' glidin
like mad hawks—swoopin black with arms
for wings, palmin the sun, throwin it down,
and even with the day gone, without even
a crumb of light from the city, *brothers*
keep runnin-gunnin, fallin away takin
fall-away j's from the corner, their bodies
like muscular saxophones *body-boppin*
better than jazz, beyond summer, beyond
weather, beyond everything that moves—
an' with one shake they're pullin-up
from the perimeter, shakin-bakin,
brothers be sweet pullin-up from
the edge a' the world, hangin like
air itself hangs in the air,
an' gravidy gotta giv'em up: the ball
burning like a fruit with a soul
in their velvet hands, while the wrists
whisper backspin, *an' the fingers comb the rock*
once—givin it up, lettin it go, lettin it go

like good news because the hoop is a well,
a well with no bottom, *an' they're*
fillin that sucker up!

THE GOOD CITY

I am weighed down by what I
didn't say to you. I
am like some fat man dragging
the moon on a rope. I could have said,
*Woman, no word can hold the letters
your body writes on my soul,*
but I didn't, so now people see me coming
and want to get their houses
out of the way, but my stone is
so much wider than America. In fact,
my head is growing another head just
to hold what I almost said that Sunday.

Everyone laughs at my trouble
though my hands tremble
like the eyes of someone ready
to beg. They say it's my fault—
they say I have that crabby, bedraggled look
of a man whose life is made of things
almost done. I should have told you
about your eyes, about the bright street
I saw in the left one and the sailfish
schooling the bay of the right.
Maybe you would have taken me home,
taken my pulse, taken me upstairs.

But it's late now, you're
somewhere in San Antonio, tugging
at crabgrass in your garden, probably
singing "Besa Me Mucho"
into the cool head of a tulip
while I've got this moon that leaves
the nation flat as buttered toast
behind me—this moon I tow like some
lame hippopotamus on a leash.

I did say, "Your dress is pretty"
but the words came stiffly
as though each were wearing
patent leather shoes, as if
my hands weren't heavy as God
with aching to touch, as if
my thin heart had been smoked
and stubbed out like a cigarette.

So today I have an extra head
that listens only to my fingers,
that hears clearly the ten nervous basses
when their sudden chorus fills my blood
with this humming, and soon
I will grow one more for remembering
that transparent door in the air,
the whispered dance of your body
beneath that yellow dress,
your hair, your silver-blue eyes—
the good city whose streets I
would wander watching you and the water
with my soul bowed like a cello.

YOU DAMN RIGHT

So much light
from one star, and tree shadows
painted on the backs
of squirrels, and one grackle throwing
his meanest voice, an evil one-
man-band with whistles, broken
cymbals and a snuffly
nose, marching back and up scolding
the grass and anyone who passes,
his blue-black bright
as a bad mood on a beautiful day—
like the day he tapped he
chiseled his way out of that
bitter egg to find the sky
a new color too far
away, and his mother stuffing who-
knows-what into his mouth
into his mouth into his mouth and
what was she always squawking about—
about how careful he needed
to be, about the world being impossible
to believe; then the sudden *So long,*
good luck, that bird foot in the butt, him
scrambling for his wings, the green
earth jumping up with all
its jagged teeth, his shoulders
burning as he tried the steep
ladder of air, feathers like
fingers clawing at what appeared
to be nothing at all,
like the light
filling up his eyes and him,
blacker than any five
good nights sewn together;
how could he have known
what would be required? How

could he know what a
cat was, what a cloud was, what
a man was—and lightning and
heartburn and hard-falling
sleet? And time
slipping past like a friend
who owes you money, like a
burglar with all your
brand new stuff; and how did he
fit into the scheme anyway,
and if he really didn't
What in the **hell**
was he doing? Of course,
he's pissed off and *you*
damn right he gonna cop
an attitude and nobody
better say shit about it
neither.

BADDER

On the corner four
black boys hurl their
fists like rocks
against each others'
chests. One of the old-heads
looks and grins. They think
they are *badder*
than bad, holding the
corner, shirtless, skin
slick as slate, eyes
like blades cutting
the hard lines of Philly—
"Aw, pussy, you can't hit."
"Oh yeah? Nigga, whatchu gon do
talkin all that shit?"
And the welts rise
like red moons with each
bang of fist. This
makes them brothers and
later they grind that
slow grind slow
against the night and sing
"Vanessa!" when she
brings her skin-tight, blue-
jeaned fine strut by
the corner.

TREATISE

Those mornings when your body refuses the call
for posture, and your blood slimes through your veins
like a great slug on its one sticky foot,
you might think about the stupid things we have to do
in trying simply to touch—how the body
always understands, while the mind is so stuffed
with half-luck and cold gravy
that often you talk to no one but yourself.

Who hasn't known that long conversation
in which nothing is said, but everything is meant,
where the first-date-clumsy silence
is really hope for a slow stroke on the arm
or a sweet invitation of eyes, but for some reason
you just keep talking then go home
wearing a glum smile like a third shoe and mumbling
what you might've said—the *abracadabra*
that would've changed the night into a sloppy kiss.

Can your body be blamed as it lies there knowing
each day will probably be like the rest:
you will see someone you want to touch, but you won't.
You won't because the mind always goes back
to the goofy routine—just as your eyes come to her
laced in the soft haze of a sexual dream,
your mind puts on its big shoe
and twirls the little cane: you walk by
like a duck while she does the same. When
you should've said, *Let's do it standing up*
before age can deface us. Let's cook it good'n'slow
before life's dumb mistakes can erase us.

Sometimes I feel my penis,
like a prisoner in solitary confinement,
raking his rusty cup against the hard bars

of this life pleading for a woman
whose name I don't even know—a genuine pleading
as though for the secret to a secret
that's been kept ever since the first sperm serenaded
the pinkness of the womb and coaxed an egg
to come out and play.

Don't you have to wonder who thought up the steps
for this grumpy parade? Because this world
shouldn't be ridiculous. What remains buried in dreams
and under these wonderful clothes, the blood
can never forget. So, those low mornings when light sags
and your lungs seem broken, remember: the good kiss
is always better than the rest of the date—
the tongue itself, far superior
to the words it shapes. Get up.

MEEP

I used to root for the rabbit
in his sneaky quest for that fruity cereal—
"Raspberry red, Lemon yellow, Orange orange"—
and I hated those big-headed little brats,
especially the boy when he'd say,
"Silly rabbit, Trix are for kids."
I always wished he'd smile *Okay, one bowl
won't hurt*, because it really wouldn't have.
I used to console myself believing
the silly rabbit swiped a bunch
between commercials.

And I used to cross my fingers
for the Coyote too—sometimes, running
like a maniac, his legs bulging from
ACME muscle builder, he'd get so close
I could feel the Road-Runner's tail feathers
tickling his nose, but suddenly "Meep meep!"
and the road was smoke all the way
to the horizon. The Coyote seemed
so ruined, the way he'd knot his brow
while his pointed face went slack.
I would shake my head and wonder
if he ever got to eat anything ever—
and why didn't he give up on that bird
or occasionally go for something slow?

Being six or seven, I guess I understood
the difference between cartoons and my life,
though I admit I couldn't figure out
why they never talked about needing
to go to the bathroom: even the wise
Mr. Peabody must've had to wet a tree
sometime, and Sherman
was a little boy like me.

It's amazing the way I believed so well
in the world—that basically
it was a place to live happily
ever after, that the only hard part
was waiting to get old enough
to stay up late and go outside
whenever you wanted. I don't know
about the world anymore—it doesn't
look like anybody actually gets
what he wants. But last Saturday
I was watching cartoons with my niece,
and when the Coyote started gaining
on the fast-assed little bird, I leaned
forward in my seat just enough
to catch myself feeling hopeful.

A JITTERBUG FOR SPRING

All along the lake the larks
send their sweet scat through the air.
It's April. New weather jazzes the leaves.
The late sun—a long note blown
across the water. Near shore
a tadpole itching for legs.

SOON

for Carlo Pezzimenti

Not even in the grave will it be this quiet

the smell of sunlight   the sparkle of children
the folding of air as someone walks through it

I listen but I don't hear anything
like this noise gathered inside my teeth

I want to say that soon someday
we'll all be underground

and the earth will not be warm

I think right now we should hold on
to each other   and tell the stories
till our hearts melt like mints in our mouths

but here come the happy shoppers with their silver crosses
their TV-hugging eyes their heads stuffed with fish

Sometimes I can hear the blood
singing in my arms

and there is no sound for the dead

Like right now with the sun broken and the slow
colors of dusk long shadows in your eyes

you can almost remember what you
were thinking   what it was that
as a child you knew   that one morning

when the plants let you watch as they began to grow

When I lie down at last   when they finally shut the lid
all I know will be found in the head of a match

I wish I could open the secret right now

that says why we can't keep letting each other die like this

ALMOST

No wind   Whole days go by
and I don't remember

Under the tree pile the acorns
and their brown caps

Where is it now

I mark down what words I can
for this   Heat ripe enough

to sit like a peach
on my shoulder   Sometimes
I almost see how it was

And faces of people I've loved

appear where just before
I saw glass scattered in the street
Where is it now

When I was a boy I would

blow on my hand and watch very closely

to see if I could see the air

SLOW DANCE

for Savannah

Some days I can go nearly an hour
without thinking of the taste
of your mouth. Right now, I'm at school
watching teenagers fidget through a test.
Outside, the sky is smoky and streets are wet
and two grackles step lightly in yellow grass.

Two weeks ago in Atlantic City
I stood on the boardwalk
and looked out across the water—
the railing was cool, broken shells
dappled the beach—I had been
playing the slot machines
and lost all but a dollar. I
tried to picture you in Paris,
learning the sound of your new country
where, at that moment, it was already night.

I thought maybe you'd be out
walking with the street lights
glossing your lips, with your eyes
deep as this field of water.
Maybe someone was looking at you
as you paused under the awning
of a bakery where the smell
of newly risen bread buttered the air.

I remember those suede boots
you wore to the party last December,
your clipped hair, your long arms
like the necks of swans. I remember
how seeing the shape of your mouth
that first time, I kept staring
until my blood turned to rain.

Some things take root
in the brain and just don't
let go. We went to
a movie once—I think
it was "The Dead"—and
near the end a woman
told a story about a boy
who used to sing: how, at 17,
she loved him, how that
same year he died. She
remembered late one night
looking out to the garden
and he was there   calling her
with only the slow sound
in his eyes.

Missing someone is like hearing
a name sung quietly from somewhere
behind you. Even after you know
no one is there, you keep looking back
until on a silver afternoon like this
you find yourself breathing just enough
to make a small dent in the air.

Just now a student, an ivory-colored girl
whose nose crinkles when she laughs, asked me
if she could "go to the bathroom,"
and suddenly I knew I was old enough
to never ask that question again.

When I look back across my life,
I always see the schoolyard—
monkey-bars, gray asphalt, and one huge tree—
where I played the summer days into rags.
I didn't love anybody yet, except maybe
my parents who I loved mainly when they

left me alone. I used to have wet dreams
about a girl named Diane. She was a little
older than me. I wanted to kiss her so bad
that just walking past her house
I would trip over nothing but the chance
that she'd be on the porch. Sometimes
she'd wear these cut-off jeans, and
a scar shaped like an acorn shone
above her knee. In some dreams I would
barely touch it, then explode. Once

in real life, at a party on Sharpnack Street
I asked her to dance a slow one with me.
The Delfonics were singing *I'll never
hear the bells* and, scared nearly blind,
I pulled her into the sleepy rhythm
where my body tried to explain.
But half-a-minute deep into the song
she broke my nervous grip and walked away—
she could tell I didn't know
what to do with my feet. I wonder
where she is now   and all those people
who saw me standing there
with the music filling my hands.

Woman, I miss you, and some afternoons
it's all right. I think of that lemon drink
you used to make and the stories—
about your grandmother, about the bees
that covered your house in Africa, the nights
of gunfire, and the massing of giant frogs
in the rain. I think about the first time
I put my arm around your shoulder. I think
of couscous and white tuna, that one lamp
blinking on and off by itself, and those plums
that would brood for days on the kitchen counter.

I remember holding you against the sink,
with the sun soaking the window, the soft call
of your hips, and the intricate flickers
of thought chiming your eyes. Your mouth,
like a Saturday. I remember your
long thighs, how they
opened on the sofa, and the pulse
of your cry when you came, and
sometimes I miss you
the way someone drowning
remembers the air.

I think about these students
in class this afternoon, itching
through this hour, their bodies new
to puberty, their brains streaked
with grammar—probably none of them
in love, how they listen to my voice
and believe my steady, adult face,
how they wish the school day would
hurry past, so they could start
spending their free time again, how
none of them really understands
what the clock is always teaching
about the way things disappear.

THE MOTION

Ah, but the spirit moves in physical ways—
the wind swims a field, a teenaged girl grins
slow and sly, and what steady ruckus does the blood make
running the body's blind streets.

The afternoon is a big house sprung with minutes.
Light chimes on a woman's bright brown hair.
Her strong calves whisper; my heart sings
like a bruise—luck spins like a june-bug crazed

by what glad music—it must be the sky bringing
sky, it must be a tribe of ants whistling
at a crumb. Everything makes a noise,
every crooning wants an ear—everywhere I go

a woman is dressed in her own shining.
A cat lands, a little boy traps his shadow
against a fence, and the eye pins all this
with one fast hand! How can the world

be in the world? My skin grown loose
as a brood of birds, I could fly
out of myself—naked, the soul would be
less than a word: a web of air, a

grabbing without fingers,
but the spirit moves in physical ways
and with it rises this righteous fever.

This slight tickling, this light madness—
it's just the dust of a day blown dim.
Night swings its tail.

DEUCE

for Ed Kennedy

It's amazing how badly we play this game at times—
the short dinker   slapped into the net,
the weak lob   clubbed all the way to the fence.
I start to wonder why I'm out here
ruining my day—

       the trees don't care
that we sweat and call ourselves names, the sun
doesn't even blink, enough is already wrong
with my life, and my forehand has grown
mysterious—I think either end
of the racket will do.

       Then you send that
hard cross-court drive top-spinning
just west of my reach and I've got
to say *Yes* to the invisible
stripe it leaves in the air
       and on my next serve
I slice heavy, I mean for that ball
to be grease when it hits
     but you've got the answer and
I'm caught leaning, my white sneaks
locked for that long second, a curse
clenched between my teeth
like a bb.

     Nothing else matters
like this, this pressing ourselves
to be true to every moment
on the court, begging the eyes to teach
exactly what we have to do,
to do it right, to place the ball inside
the edges but beyond hope.
    This bright-green ball, the one word

the rackets say over and over,
the argument between two men, running
it down, trying to come back
with the insight that
settles everything.

               Or maybe the ball is music
and we can't help but move to it,
the way Saturday is music to children,
calling them outside to chase around
and around the block beyond their
ever knowing why—

               your shot inviting me
to shake a leg or lose the rhythm, my shot
taking you wide with the sweet spot strings
ringing that short minor chord, me
watching you invent the steps—

          getting there   getting it   getting it back—
                    the feet
faster than the sound,
the torso turning into the rhythm, arms
swinging, the blood quick, the body
covering the court chasing the heat climbing
the sun's hard stare.

               If we didn't have these
rackets, brother, if we didn't
have to worry about the lines, if
the ball were really invisible
and this was the green
slope of a grassy hill scored white by milkweed,
with the whole blue ocean of sky
tossed perfectly above us

               wouldn't this be
     a wild day

wouldn't this be
the right dream
                wouldn't we be   dancing

TO THE MOVIES

It's Saturday afternoon. In matinees
all over America popcorn tumbles
into the huge mouths of children.
They are all watching the same show—
a lady in love with a man in love
with a car. It's not easy to tell
what the kids think, but you know
they are happy, surrounded by parents
and darkness, the distinct call
of splitting cellophane, and the sweet
brown ice at the bottoms of empty Cokes.

Looking at their faces, row after row
burning in movie-light, you might try
to remember what it was to throw yourself
into long, unstoppable throbs of laughing
and why a car's wheezy song is so funny.

It is hard to believe the movie will end
with all the characters so ready
to spend the endless happily-ever-after
and how, walking back up the aisles
with the bright music behind them,
the children will be a little sad
and, in some ways, more willing to
swallow disappointment. But you know
it must be true when you think of
your life—thirty years drawn by
the marquee as though by another chance,
your large head resting weightless
as memory   on the warm skin of your hand.

MOMENTUM

I'm on a roll

Everywhere I look   there's something

Over there for example

My father used to hold his pipe just like that

But not really I guess

I'm still on a roll though
even though life isn't as clear as it seems

Like this morning

I dreamt I was running up these wooden stairs
while my mom slept in a cream-colored convertible parked on
      the lawn

I don't know what it means

But I know weather when I see it
Nobody has to tell me it's partly cloudy

I haven't watched news for weeks

In the rest of America things could be happening

People could be   for example   misbehaving

Acting like stupid racist homophobic warmongering sexist
violent environmentally insane greedy assholes

Someone could be saying, "Hey, don't be like that."

And maybe everybody's telling you-know-who

to **cram it**

But you never know

Ninth grade we used to sit in the back row and see
who could say *cram it* the loudest without getting caught

The key was a deeper voice because the shrieks always made
        everybody turn around

I know Mr. Stafileadis hated us
He wanted to teach history
But we were on a roll

Packed tight with hormones like mailboxes near Christmas
tight like that   like hampers crammed full of grimy
        play clothes

I don't like to get nostalgic

I'd rather just talk like one of the fellas
say it just like it comes—say
Put that in your pipe and smoke it

like a roofer

But when you're on a roll

you gotta give yourself to history

let it elbow around in your guts like somebody tough

until if you don't open your mouth and spill everything

your front teeth'll get punched clean out

WHAT IT COMES DOWN TO

for James Mardis

Eyes shining that half-sane stare,
T-shirts ripped with sweat—Dewey and Zack
one-on-one in Zang Park: a second ago
they climbed the air, new Nikes
laced loose, dark blue, stole three feet of sky,
and Dewey spit, "Gaah-damn!"
when his finger-roll spun off the rim.

August spins the breeze to wool, the late sun
melts like butter. Somebody says, "Zack gonna,
Zack gonna bust the bottom out now,"
and a car radio thumps bass, but the real
beat is a basketball banging concrete
and two tall brothers blowing hard.

All summer they'd been *talkin that talk*
about who had the moves, who ruled the lane,
who had the angel's kiss on the shot—
this was the championship of the park.

Just one more bucket, just one sweet J
and Zack goes home with the game
like a jewel in his heart. "Yo, Dew,"
yells a boy with a penny's worth of hair,
"you know Z ain' nothin' but money
lef' side a'the key." Across the street

three men play poker: one hums
a slow run from a blues and, seeing
the two boys glistening sweat, remembers
when he could glide the air, could
"damn near rub his nose on the rim,"
those summers spent under the trees
cooling between games, how the fellas
used to call him "Sky," and the girls

used to call him sweet—right there,
right there in the park   while

the ball bounces back   back   and back
with Dewey flexed low, one hand on Zack
the other pawing toward the dancing rock.
Night makes its move, its smooth black hand
palming the earth.

Sometimes, everything you want
comes down to one shot, one perfect play
on a street where forty years
can steal your legs and leave you holding
two wrong cards. Sometimes
the only thing that makes sense
is the right kiss of fingertips
against a ball too sweaty to grip,
when your body aches like a wish
above the city and a splash of fire
opens your eyes. All over the Southside
brothers lace their sneaks and smolder
for a little luck to see by: Zack

                    fakes right
                skips the pill left   spins
        rises   pumps   hangs
                and falls into the dark, shooting.

II. Appetite

ONE

Dishes in the sink

Outside, the sky, a fat man in grey—
a big bag of rain on his back

Thoughts in my head like a family
of rats

Like centipedes under a rock

Late June and light across
this page

The lamp never forgets what to do
Last night I dreamed
someone

was biting me on the face

Voices from the alley—two boys
with a pellet gun trying to kill something—

Look   Look   There one is

AFTER ALL

Let's say you're black and you walk in
this restaurant and as you take your seat you
realize you're the only one there darker
than blue—the waiters and waitresses, the hostess
and customers, even the cooks; all of them
could walk into a snowy field and vanish—so
you think *No big deal, it's cool, no need to*
get into a Frederick Douglass kinda thing . . .
But soon the peekaboo sets in: you
look up from buttering a roll and notice
a middle-aged woman combing your face
like a gutsy, low-flying pilot
on reconnaissance and another lady with a
headful of gray, greenish-gold, highlit hair
begins snapping her glance at you and away, at you
and away, as if some kind of suggestive cucumber
were slowly emerging from your forehead and only
she can see it. The one old, bald, Burl Ives-
looking guy just stares at you with something
between a grimace and a yawn stuck on his face.
Yeah, and you know he'd love to break
into a little "Jimmy Crack Corn and I Don't Care"
with his fat little lobster-colored neck extending
and retracting, his thumbs pinned under his arms,
elbows flapping, knees wobbling—Goddammit!

Now you start to feel weird; you scrutinize
your fork for evidence that someone sneezed on it.
Don't get a kink in the gut, you say to yourself,
closing your eyes, breathing deeply. *After all,*
what's with all this paranoia? "Kareem Abdul-Jabbarrr!"
the waiter grins, refilling your water, "you
look a lot like'im." And you can't remember
anybody black ever telling you that. You
imagine this guy trying to fall asleep

some nights counting black men floating above
some bright parquet floor, dunking   sky-hooking,
sky-hooking   dunking. You begin to wonder
why your food is taking so long. You recall
stories of the **New** South—brothers testing
the waters of once segregated diners and
getting served entrees garnished with
garbage and spit. After all, there's nothing
that suggests these people marched
on Washington in '63, these sausage-headed cooks
in particular. There's no air of the former
Freedom Rider about **any** of these porcelain-colored
characters who blink and nod at each other,
carving their meat into some kind of code.
After all, who was heckling the people
who made the Selma trek with King—somebody
was shouting *Niggers, go home!* and
feeling good about it. Maybe here they are,
a bunch of *somebodies* out for dinner,
and here you are, crashing the party, a
coffee stain on the lapel of a white, white
tuxedo, a kinky hair floating in a glass
of milk, and here comes your food, your waiter
carrying it high above his head. "Ka-reem,"
he says, "sorry it's taken so long, Kareem—
bet you can't wait."

DOGS

for Eduardo Galeano

Dogs know things.

They know the important things come from a person's head.

That's why they look at your face when you're giving
    commands.

They hear what you say.

They know what time you said you'd take'em for a walk.
They know.

They see people throwing voices back and forth.
They see you and your pals looking at each other talking.

They see the anchor people burping out news on TV.
They see you watching.

They hear your face bending around sentences.
They see you wink. They know you know they can't
wink back at you.

Dogs know stuff.

They know their names are not *their* names.

And they get tired of hearing **NO!** all the time.

They know you know you shouldn't stare into their eyes.

Dogs don't wanna play around all the time.

They know you "throw ball" and do "jump for the treat"
because you feel funny about being mean sometimes.

They know that alotta days you wish they'd shut-up and just
    STAY!
They know who gets hit with the newspaper.
They know that you know it doesn't matter if they mind.

Dogs know stuff about things.

They know about those *No Dogs Allowed* signs.

They know who domesticated who. They know
who pets who whenever whoever feels like it. They know
who keeps whose food shut up in the pantry
next to the broom.

They know who bred who into long-legged, goofy-looking
    afghan hounds.
They know who bred who into cute-little, nasty, yip-yapping
    fur balls.
They know who takes who to get whose ears cropped.

Dogs know who gets who "fixed."

Wagging a tail is not always a happy sign.

You know how sometimes certain muscles twitch
when certain other muscles wanna be kickin' somebody's ass,

how sometimes you nod your head and say *that's okay,*
while your left hand keeps cramping into a fist.

Dogs deal with   things like this.

They know who gets locked up in the garage.
They know who doesn't get to dig in the garden.
They know who has to shit in public.
They know who puts who "to sleep."

SHAPE

for the A.N.C.

The P.A. tells someone to
pick up a courtesy phone and I
almost do because in an airport
you can be everybody
                but today
I am the assassin
looking for the President
of South Africa. My hat shadows
my face like a sneer.
                   I have
a blow-gun
made from the hollow body
of a *Bic* and one dart tipped
with the piss
of an angel
so angry that even God
sits down when she dances.

The brothers see me
and nod, not blinking. The
black women mouth promises
of big-legged nights, slyly
proffering plum-colored
lips between which their
smiles splash like tambourines.

His flight is unloading at gate six—
his escorts mutter Afrikaans
between constipated
grins and glances.
               Then, like a
cavity in a tooth,
he appears. He is thinking
about his wife's white
neck in the windswept nights

of Pretoria. In the bathroom
his men check each stall. His
right hand lands
on his zipper. Outside jets
rip into the sky.

When the door marked **MEN** opens
I am kissing
the silver curl rising
from the fountain.
                    He pats his hands
on his coat. I lift the pen
palming it
so only the tip shows—
my first knuckle under my nose, I
could be covering a cough or
yawning
            as a tangle of workmen, kids,
parents and priests
scuffle by. Half-steady,
half-afraid
like a snake charmer watching
his first cobra climb
into the air, I blow:
                    one little boy
thinks he saw a bee—a woman with
ragged red hair nearly catches
death in her mouth—the shoeshine man
says something skimmed his cheek
while the president

takes two short steps
and leans into history.
                    The bodyguards
wheel, hearts wagging in their throats,
guns glistening
in the airport jumble
but I'm already

                    everyone else
already another shape
in a crowd
waiting to fly.

FACULTY MEETING

I will draw
a buck-toothed man's grinning face
on the side of this dixie cup.
I will be sitting
in a very important professional meeting
doing this.

You will say to me
that I am childish
and should pay attention
to the several obvious facts
that the speaker is pointing out.

I will ask you
to repeat
what you just said.

You will.

I will write "Fuck Yourself"
underneath the buck-toothed man's
friendly face
and turn it toward you.

You will take away
my dixie cup
and ball it up
with a mature disgust. And
you will expect me
to understand
that this
is not the time
or place. But

I will not understand.
I will begin to drag you

around the meeting-room floor
by your stupid, skinny, blue tie.

You will express that
it is difficult to breath
and that you cannot believe
I'm doing this
on a Thursday—with Friday so
close at hand, with the weekend
beaconing like a beach.

I will insist that you
taste the heel of my right shoe
by wedging it in your mouth
like a licorice. For a moment

your eyes will reflect
the gritty flavor. Then
you will become desperate to
speak to clarify to reconcile to
reconsider—then
you will be sleeping.

I will uncrumple my dixie cup
and wave the grinning
buck-toothed face like a flag
before all of my learned colleagues.

They will make note
of the profane inscription
shining beneath the goofy chin
on the cup. They will understand that this
buck-toothed face of a paper man
without hope, a woman
or even a chance to work
is like a god to me.

LIKE THIS

All afternoon someone watches
the shadow of a branch
climb the legs of a chair,
and from someplace behind her
you can hear the scratchy whine
of a radio not quite tuned—but *climb*
is not the word; the shadow
moves like something poured, spilling
up rather than down
the wooden legs, and
though she is not
thinking exactly this
the woman knows that *climb* is not
the word—she is not
climbing out of this mood;
in fact, she is falling
to the mood just above it,
just as she fell
awake this morning—
the alarm tripping her up
into the world, the sudden
click like a catapult, and now
from this altitude her bed
is a blurry speck, hard
even to remember: blue sheets?
striped? Her whole apartment
a tiny rectangular box
somewhere down there
where once she crossed and
uncrossed her legs, and
the woman thinks that if she
really were high up
like a jet, like someone standing
no-hands on the wing, she
would not be so

involved in the inch
by inch of shadow taking over
a chair, she would be
climbing hand over fist
through the air, using her thick
nappy hair as a rudder, thinking *why
haven't I
always lived like this,*
while all the radios in America
whimpered someplace
behind her—the simulcast news
of her defection
spilling up and filling her
blouse the way a swimmer's hand
silvers with ocean, her
strong arms turning
the beige silhouette of shore
to smoke
as she weaves the far water
into a second skin, a shadow
she can leave there like something spilled
across the floor, something like
that one there,
that one—behind you,   climbing.

STORIES

I'll probably never die.
My life will just go on and on,
on days like this especially.
All of my life will be composed of days
where nobody in my city kisses or makes love,
days where a single black-winged butterfly
bothers a tall blue spruce,
where the air barely brushes the hair
on my wrists, where the sunlight
has nothing to do.

Sometimes I sit outside clipping my toenails,
and there's a glint of metal from a window
across the street and I think *this is how
it'll end for me*—I'll be fuckin around
with my big toe and some frustrated dentist
with a Winchester will shove me out of this life
the way some dusty kid brushes a ladybug
off his knee. Some days I can feel the crosshairs
settling on a spot just behind my ear, the bullet
clearing one thin path through the wind: it's
afternoon, the smell of exhausts oils the air.
I see myself tipping over with this skinny river
of music inside my head, but I'm still here—
as far as I can see backwards, there I am
with this gang of hours growing behind me.

When I was about nine
two teenaged guys, Lonnie and his friend
who said he had a knife, took me down
to this place near the railroad tracks.
It was summer. My father was at work.
My mom was at the *Food Fair* steering a cart
that had one of those weeble-wobbling back wheels

that got on her nerves. When we reached
the thickest bunch of trees, they stopped
and I thought I was gonna get
stabbed. Lonnie's friend said, "Drop
your pants," and when my red shorts hit
my sneakers he smiled, "Them too,"
meaning my dingy underwear with the
drunken elastic, and I stood there shrinking
with my T-shirt covering halfway to my knees.

My friends were back in the schoolyard
playing "Dead Block," sliding jelly-jar tops
across the concrete, trying to get
to the twelfth box, trying not to land
on the skull in the middle, probably
not thinking of me at all. I thought
about how I wouldn't want to be found
dead without my pants on, how my parents
would be ashamed. "Lift up the shirt," he said
and there I was, scared to death
with my thimble-sized jammy bald as a minnow,
while they laughed and pretended they were gonna
take my clothes and tie me to the tracks.

I won't ever die. I'm positive—especially
on days like this when I'm not even sure
if I'm sad or just a little run-down. Especially
when the chinaberry tree keeps letting one
pale yellow leaf fall, and up on a telephone wire
a mourning dove repeats five fluting sounds,
as if even that perfect sentence could explain
a single moment of this life.

I admit I wanted my body to be a saxophone—
I thought the air wanted to be music
and I wanted to make love like a sizzling angel,
like some sort of jazz god whose every note
was a glyph in the alphabet of fire—all the time.

And time grew up all around me while I just
talked and waited.

Once, I got kicked out of World History
for talking in the back row of class. Mr.
Groobie told me to shut-up, so I
stuffed my chest with *bad-ass* and said,
"What're you gonna do if I don't?"
It felt good to feel the class swell behind me
to watch the teacher turn red and shrink.
But by the time I got home I just knew
nothing I could say would stop my father.
I went up to my room. It was around 3:30.
My father worked till five. I remember
watching the second-hand glide—the fear
filling me up as though I'd been swallowing
those ragged undershirts my mother used
for dusting. I thought maybe if I was
outside raking when he drove in, things might
go better—or maybe if I was studying
in the living room when he opened the door.
The clock's face seemed almost sorry
when the screen scraped open and his key
cracked the lock. I only wanted to be dead
before my mother gave him the news, before
I had to straddle that black chair
in the basement, before I saw him
snatch off his belt.

I bet my life will drift on and on
like some kind of blind fish that
can't really figure out where it is—
on days like this especially, especially
with dusk rising out of the earth
like a woman slowly waking to the noise
of girls chanting jump-rope hymns—
all over lightning bugs and their tiny lanterns,
the blood in my brain full of phosphorus like bay water.

I envy the dead their worry-free days—
no more roaches in the kitchen, no bigots,
nobody smirking at your shoes, no more
waiting for some bonehead to call you back,
nobody wondering if you're married, no bills, no
changing your mind or needing a shower or wincing
at someone's sultry strut, no music for
setting the mood, no one to meet for lunch,
nobody stealing your wallet, no reason to be
nervous, no more mosquito bites, no allergies,
no Presidents, no nausea, no bad weather, and no more news
about people dying—but I'd rather be above ground
running the weeks always coming back
to Monday   *Mon- -day*   like two notes
some crazed bird coos as it circles your life.

Sometimes, with the right morning, I go out.
I let the rain spell my body, and I think
about the stories, how they shine inside us,
how they must come together somewhere
and make no sense at all, but rather remind us
that once upon a time, we were real,
that all kinds of stuff happened,
and the result was our lives.

I was riding the XH bus to Germantown
Lutheran Academy—early spring I guess.
I was feeling a little blah because my parents
made me eat cream of wheat for breakfast
when I just wanted some cinnamon toast. Then,
at Washington Lane, a mob of Germantown High babes
got on. I was standing by the automatic door
halfway to the back, feeling more and more
like the private school eighth-grader I was,
when this really foxy white girl crowds in
sorta beside me, sorta in front of me. She's
wearing these red fish-net stockings and a
black mini-skirt, and her hair was brown sneaking

toward blond. I had on my **GLA** blazer
and this cornball silver-green tie. She
smelled like strawberries and cigarettes.
At the next stop another bunch of people crammed in,
and suddenly her right hip was set firmly against
my left. I believed she would move to open
a small space between us, and when she didn't this
queaziness, like a flock of winged mice,
claimed me from belly to throat.

Until then, my only interracial moment
consisted of rubbing Karen Goldsmith's calf
on the pretense of touching the reddish birthmark
behind her knee. So, being a weaselly little horntoad
of 13 with the vapors of smoke and fruit hazing my soul,
I eased my body bit by tiny bit leftward, holding
my breath until my jammy replaced my hip
against her—at which point she moved
smooth as a minute hand to the right.

That feeling, that feeling when I knew that she knew
she had pinned her butt gently against me—
well, I think about it sometimes now, especially
on days like this when the sidewalk is stoked
with summer and all the ants are running, when
no one in my city can be bothered with a kiss,
especially on days like this when I'm
right in the middle of living forever,
and a crowded bus blunders past and I see
the people packed inside pretending they
don't really see each other, pretending
they aren't seriously dying
to taste that strange communion, to feel that
nearly accidental spark pressed into their skin.

NATASHA IN A MELLOW MOOD

(apologies to Bullwinkle and Rocky)

Boris, dahlink, look
at my legs, long
as a lonely evening in Leningrad,
how they open the air
when I walk, the way moonlight
opens the dark. Boris, my hair
is so black with espionage,
so cool and quiet with all those secrets
so well kept—those secret plans
you've nearly kissed
into my ears. Who gives a proletarian
damn about Bullwinkle and that
flying squirrel and that idiot
who draws us? America
is a virgin, the cartoonist who leaves me
less than a Barbie doll under
this dress, who draws me
with no smell—**he** is a virgin.
The children who watch us
every Saturday mornink
are virgins. Boris, my sweet waterbug, I
don't want to be a virgin anymore.
Look into my eyes, heavy
with the absence of laughter
and the presence of vodka. Listen
to my Russian lips muss up
these blonde syllables of English:
Iwantchu. Last night
I dreamed you spelled your
code name on my shoulder
with the waxed sprigs of your
moustache. I had just come
out of the bath. My skin was still
damp, my hair poured like ink

as I pulled the comb through it. Then
I heard you whisper, felt you take
my hand—Oh, Boris, Boris
Badenov, I want your mischief-
riddled eyes to invent
my whole body, all the silken
slopes of flesh forgotten
by the blind cartoonist. I want
to be scribbled all over you
in shapes no pencil would dare. Dahlink,
why don't we take off
that funny little hat. Though
you are hardly tall
as my thighs, I want your pointy
shoes beside my bed, your
coat flung and fallen
like a double-agent
on my floor.

BORIS BY CANDLELIGHT

Natasha, first this—
then what? I'll be looking
into the shadows and, instead
of that buck-toothed squirrel, I'll see
your body drawn like an ivory blade
slicing the dark. Then what good
will I be to Fearless Leader?
All of Moscow will become your
slow walk, as though the entire city
swam with your slim thighs
shortening the streets.

Natasha, we are supposed to be
comrades in the struggle—we are
supposed to be taking the world
back from America. We should be nabbing
Rocky and giving him some convincing
bonks on the head. But don't think
I haven't noticed your blouse
ripe as midnight when you pass by
at headquarters, and that sleepy
invitation in your glance when
we've been spying too long
in the White House basement,
squinting into that small
circle of light.

Once   I saw the wind turn around
in your raven hair and thought
of your dress as a full sail and
myself, a small island upon which you
might be shipwrecked for an evening.
Do you really think that when I
close my eyes it's Bullwinkle
that haunts the dim hall inside me?

But, dahlink, we are supposed to be
dreaming of a more perfect State.

You must understand, Natasha,
in every frame of this life
we invent ourselves and the air.
The cartoonist is just a sad rumor,
like the distance you see between us.
These lines that shape our bodies,
that separate us and break up the world—
they're there because you think
they're there. You have always been
a part of me, Natasha. I have
already sketched you a million times
with my soul's invisible ink.
I love you as much as I live
for Russia. But these capitalists,
baby, they will snatch even the broken moon
if we look away and let them.

THE BALLAD OF SADIE LABABE

Sadie LaBabe   was a magic sister
Lord, even a blind man   couldn'a missed'er
Her sultry skin   was dark as shade
Her mind cut sharp as a butcher's blade
And the brothers who stared   at Sadie's thighs
Would shake their heads and moan and cry

'Cause Sadie moved like water poured
The shapes she shaped had angels floored
She knew her walk turned wind to fire
A wink from Sadie turned brains to mire

The mellow fellas tried to talk that sly
They'd high-sing "Sadie!" when she walked by
But if she stopped   to pass some time
Their lines went stale   and sank to slime
She yawned she'd heard it   all before—
Stuff bad boys write on bathroom doors

'Cause Sadie pours like rivers move
Her black skin rocks men toward the blues
She won't be mine, she won't be yours
She bit Eve's apple down to the core

Now J.T. Kade   was Billy-Dee handsome
His humble home they called *Love Mansion*
He was ice cream cool   and built like a panther
Whatever the question   J.T. was the answer.
The sisters crowned him King of The Land
He could make a girl faint just by holding her hand

So one fast day this last July
King Cool J.T. came boppin' by
Now Kade had come   from way up in Philly
His eyes were steady, his lines were chilly

He said he'd come down Dallas way
For this heavy hittin' hammer they called LaBabe

'Cause Sadie loved like honey tasted
She'd groove you till your life was wasted
Her tongue was silk, her touch was satin
She'd soothe you till your hills would flatten

But Sadie heard   what the sisters said
About this brother who broke their bread
She made the pledge, "This Saturday night
I'll be home alone by candlelight
And if this Kade   is whatch'all say
I won't mind much if he comes my way"

'Cause Sadie's heart   could hold an ocean
She moved more ways   than there was motion
Let tight be fat   and tall be low
You gonna maybe-with-Sadie, she gonna stop your show

Three days went past   and kept on goin'
By Saturday night a light breeze was blowin'
With candle-shine flecked in her eyes
Sadie sat lazy while the crickets cried
Her blouse was cotton, her shorts were suede
She had big doubts about this Kade

But from the porch there   tapped a noise
And through the screen she   caught his voice
"Say, Lady-Sadie, won'tcha let me in
I got some wine and some time to spend
I'm knockin' here 'cause I know you're there
Wanna slide my hands through your thick black hair"

So Sadie smiled   and licked her lips
Said "*Greaze* and slide under   since you're so slick
The pleasure's my treasure, we don't need no wine
I like your style   and I've heard you're fine—

Let the body be danced   and the soul be dazzled
Let's make love shapes till the stars get frazzled"

They talked awhile   then he touched her face
She twined her arm   around his waist
The chatting stopped, the kissing started
The routes they used had not been charted
They rocked the sofa, then bumped the door
They bruised the stairs, they warped the floor
The storm they raised   blew out the candles
He held her hips like they had handles
A whole day passed   and neither seemed tired
If sex is electric   this couple was wired.

So Sunday went off when Monday morning came on
Sadie stood up and stretched, but Kade was gone
The grapevine says he's in a home
For those who run   where none should roam
They say he sings, he stutters, he raves
About some lady he calls LaBabe
For him the world   has come unhinged—
He yells, "Sadie loves like a big fish swims!"
The doctors scratch their heads and frown
They drug his milk   to calm him down

While Sadie sips soda by a swimmin' pool
Her mind is clear, her skin is cool
Sometimes she feels   a little sadness
For drivin' Kade to that   sweet madness
But Sadie holds what most let fall—
"If you're gonna half-step don't step at all!"

'Cause Sadie played   in the Garden of Eden
She tamed the snake   and taught him readin'
She won't be mine, she won't be yours
She ate Eve's apple   and asked for more

C- Willms
Willams

APPETITE

I have eaten the donuts, the plain-cake,
healthy, whole wheat donuts. I have
eaten them quickly the way the highway
chews the dark licorice of Firestone tires.
I have savored the caky flavor with
a born-again gleam in my smile, with
my heart turned wild as a one-eyed pirate
with treasure on his breath. I have eaten
my way southerly and northerly and side
to side, tasting donuts from every angle
the way a blind man might try the legs
of certain women, women in blue-jean skirts
unbuttoned to mid-thigh, proud women
who stroll the blue boulevards of summer
wearing a thin glaze of sweat
like a damp halo on their labia.

I have eaten the Fig Newtons too—
all night without stopping, all night
the way witches roll moonlight like taffy
on their tongues. I did it in the kitchen.
I did it on the lawn. I did it
as though my soul were just a jaw
chewing my life into new hungers.
I attacked without reason like a great
Afro-American shark finning the crowded
streets of America—my nappy dorsal
splitting the air, the pale victims
going down fast like Fig Newtons
into a man mad for that gushy feel,
that soft cookie flavor.

And the pretzels,
those laced boomerangs of twisted bread
through which a black finger might drift

like a thunderhead through the sky's
sheer blouse. I have eaten them all
except for one, crouched like a felon
behind that bag of barbecue chips,
but he is mine. I will eat him
as surely as Europe ate South America—
just knock on his door tomorrow;
no one will answer.

And I regret nothing and I am
not sorry and I don't feel bad about
wanting so much of what I like: some days
I sit all afternoon leering at a
box of ginger snaps. Other times,
without warning, I am biting big chunks
out of something—just like Flo-Jo
yums up the meters with her big stride,
with my hands and eyes I am riding
teeth-first across this life, as if my
appetite were the only way out of this
lonely skin I'm stuck inside—
but it's late—night nibbles the city
and all the avenues cool wantonly like cakes.

III. Rain

SWEET ONION SOUP

When a man is killed
the wind doesn't cool his face
and the sky is like an urn, like
a painted bowl turned over on him.
He's so weak lying there—his hand
is like a starfish too far from the sea.
He would like to lift it up and
place it over his face to fend off
the glare of things still living.
And even if his stomach is empty
he only wants a little to eat—maybe
half-a-slice of bread and one spoonful
of sweet onion soup. Not like
when he was alive, which already seems
three Aprils ago, when he would eat
everything he could fit
into his eyes. "One time,"
his father told him, "when your cousin
turned his head to sneeze
you stole the porkchop off his plate."
But when a man is killed he
doesn't remember being a boy very much—
maybe a few things, like trying
to keep a bullfrog in a shoebox
or having to sit still in church
while his father's raised right eyebrow
flew above him like a hawk.
But he's in such a helpless mood.
His mouth is dry and he can't quite
move his tongue across his lips
which is something he used to do
all the time.

THE FAITHFUL

Where do they think *He* will lead them

Lying there the sky falling
through the holes in his hands
disappearing

When I was younger and still
hoping I was not what I am
I went to pasture

I found them nosing their chips
delighted   they showed me his name and way

The moths worshiping him
the frail light drifting from his skin
I turned to the faithful I

wanted them to know   I said *look*
but they were already holding hands
headed for the sky singing

At night
when it is too dark to see
He rises

RAIN

Take a glass of water
Pour it in the street

After awhile   it will
come back to you

from the sky
            It may be many
months   years even
but that
            April will come
that one November
with the one
small cloud
            looking for you

And even if it doesn't   even
if it never never comes
all those hours
            with your thirst
            your memory
licking the fire blue
sky   waiting
            will leave your
hard brown face
            a leaf

shining in whatever
rain there is

*the problem or
promise of
giving - the
gift that may
not - must not -
return*

THE DEBT

I have the blood of the conquerors in my veins
and the blood of the enslaved and the slaughtered,
so where shall I rest with this
mixed river of blood painting my heart—what city
wants me, which woman will touch my neck?

So the Ivory Coast is sleeping in the angles
of my skull, and maybe two small French towns,
one in each leg, are also sleeping—and of course,
the first people in this land, with their long
black, black hair, seven of them
are napping along my ribs

                              and with all these people
adrift in my body, I am asleep as well—
dreaming their good wishes, their strained whispers—
sleepwalking all over America.
But it's all right; in America everyone
is asleep: at the wheel, on the job, even
with their fingers on the trigger, asleep
with their distant continents, the glittering
silence of their shattered histories
and the long pull of a thousand
thousand moons inside them.

                              They don't remember
how once we swam inside our mothers, that
once our mothers floated inside their mothers,
just as their mothers once waited inside those
before them and before that it was the same—
all the way back to the first mother
in Africa,

              that slim, short, quick-tempered woman
whose children crawled

all over the planet, then got big and started
hurting each other—with the conquerors
in their bright armor, trying to finish everything.

I know where the blame falls. I know
I could twist my brown skin, my mixed nations, my
kinky hair into a fist. I know.   I know.

But I hear a stranger music in my bones—
the windy shimmer of long fields, the singular tree
of all blood rising, a quiet of birds stunned by dusk,
the future awake singing from these wounds, and

what is the lesson of history, if not
that we owe each other more bread, more
friendship, fewer lies,
less cruelty.

SOMETHING SILVER-WHITE

Last night
I saw the moon
and remembered the earth
is also just a rock
riding the infinite dark
wave of space—that
somewhere else
deep down in the Milky Way
someone very different
could look up from a garden
to see something silver-white
candling faintly above a hilltop
and think *that dull star seems
so weary near the rest*, not knowing

that all of us are living
on that small taste of light
buying food, calling friends,
killing each other, sleeping,
and sometimes staring back
into the speckled blackness.
You know   you can spend
your whole life
glancing at your watch
while everything mysterious
does everything mysterious
the way gravity keeps everybody
close to the ground

It *is* hard to believe this
huge, wet stone is always
flying through space—and hard
to admit there's really nothing
to hold onto   while we build houses
and fences and thousands of churches

as though this globe were just
a fat blossom atop some iron stalk
grown from God's belly.

After sailing this blue ark
so many years together
you might think
we would be kinder
because, no matter what
anybody says about
anybody else, we were all born
to this planet suddenly
blinking under the same star
and the evening sky
means the universe
is floating.

NOTES

There is the sadness of letters
waiting in mailboxes   and the sadness of words
locked in the throat   the sadness of cicadas
when summer closes   and the sadness
of the last one to ring

There is the sadness of September   the sadness
of children who can't help growing up
and the sadness of animals
that never reach the other side of the street
like the sadness of soldiers the sadness of their
captains   and the sadness in all the dead left behind

There is the sadness of trying to make it   the sad sound
of shoes hitting sidewalks   and the sadness
of the feet themselves   dreaming only
of balance   There is the sadness of a priest
watching a woman in a thin blouse   and the sadness
in the soft flesh of the mouth   like the sadness of nights
alone   the sadness in coins and dollar bills
the sadness in all the hands that hold them

There is the sadness of the Amish   whose thighs know
no jazz   and the sadness of the elderly
gathered round their TV's   and the sadness
of people   who sleep on the streets
the sad river of faces going by them

There is the sadness of scientists   who shape the weapons
of overkill   and the gleaming sadness of missiles   waiting
like letters   the sadness of dust falling
on a violin   and the sadness of marriage   the years spent
circling love   the sadness of working
the sadness of bills to be paid   always to be
paid   and the sadness of being sick and tired of it

There is the sadness of the firing squad and
the sadness of those brought blindfolded for the lullaby
of rifles   like the sadness of extinct animals and the sadness
of the fossils they will become   the sadness of time
wasted   the sadness of sighing at a clock
and the sadness of the skull   just beneath the face

like the sadness of sadness   when there are only
words   when the air is mist and
rain robes the city   and somewhere
someone sad takes notes

LARVA

Near the mountains toward evening
it is quiet. Your skin feels good
against the wind's soft hips.
Resting your head on a log
you hear a tiny larva turning over
and over, trapped in its dream
deep inside the wood.

You want to say something
about being a man, about
these handshakes men share
that bind their lives into fists.
You want to say that it is not fair
that between men there is always a plea.
You want to say what has been missing
is simple   and kiss your father's cheek.

But there is only the wind
and whatever has kept you silent
and the twilight and two blue-headed birds
nested in the crooked trestles of a bridge.
Turning back, you can see the moon
as it clears the trees   and yourself
walking among its white rocks.
You remember how looking up from the earth
it always seems small enough
to fit in your hand.

POEM

In a hundred years   I will have
forgotten this night   this
whir of traffic from the avenue

I will have forgotten
this voice   this short bridge
of words   this light scratching
at the door

Let me go down to the river
where the water is clear
I am tired of the city

In a hundred years
maybe less   I will have forgotten
the iridescent shine in the eyes
of the living   and the mind's black fire

and this windy October   this quick turning of leaves
will be a single speck of dust
in a grave   nobody visits

Friends   what rainy blues
is this   with such slow wailing
coming from my wrists

Where did I get this   stack of Mondays

I throw up my hands   and my hands
don't come back to me   not
in a hundred years either
I have already forgotten
why I needed them

just as I can no longer

remember   those nine months
inside my mother   and that
early perfection   of understanding
nothing in the world

THE LAMPS

for Joy Nolan

When you come into the room
huge fish turn underwater

and I feel the lamps
come on in my wrists

I fold my hands I   close my eyes
Your hair falls   from April
to December
dark as a forest in a rainstorm

Once   when we danced to slow music
I found the end of a day   risen
like a staircase inside me

the evening sky hung purple-black
and tucked into the steep side of a hill two houses
each with a lamp
turning the porch pale gold

I could hear a stream nearby
and the sound of someone   talking to the shallows

Woman   I wish I could tell you
what the water said
about the weather
in your smile   the way the late hours
spill their music   over your mouth

Where I am now   there is no sound
but my own   slow thinking
and sometimes the air
trying to understand the wind

What question have you pressed into my blood

that I can't help
but answer

      When you walk by
   your long shadow
             rings   like a moonrise

EACH LETTER

When a woman is killed
the cicadas go looking for their shells
and put them on again and climb
back into the earth and the year
returns to February. And if
the air is chilly
she feels it—in fact, if you
put your hand on her arm
you would know she still remembers
how touching changed the weather,
how a hand skimming the wrist
was once a window
opening onto a better season
where people did better things
than be lonely, where the wind
was a river of candlelight
pushing the blue silhouettes of trees.
It doesn't matter that everyone
thinks she feels nothing—in fact,
she prefers it like that because
more than anything else, right now,
she feels tired and would like
a moment to herself
while she tries to remember
the name of her sister.
But each letter is so heavy
that carrying a whole word
to the front of her mind
is hard, so she stays there
remembering the warmth of honey
between her toes, with her blood
not humming, with the sound
of the name always almost coming to her.

GRAFFITI

Probably by the end of the day
they'll find me squashed under a truck,
an eighteen-wheeler probably—one
of them old dusty ones with license plates
from every state quilted below the grill
or, better yet, under one of them
mud-brown **UPS** trucks that look like a
Frankenstein head on wheels—yeah,
I'll be under the left front tire
mished like a moth in the mouth of a cat.

And everything had been looking up too—
tomorrow I bet someone was gonna
start liking me in that certain way
that leads to kisses so deep that all
your vital organs get shuffled around,
kisses that leave you breathing out your knees.
And she would've been Ethiopian too, with
that wavy black hair, with them mother-midnight eyes
and one of them serious accents that make you wanna
walk all the way back to the first splash
of the Nile, that make you wanna graffiti her
name all over the city in saliva.

But it really doesn't matter now, now
that some blind bus driver's already
caught my scent. I don't know how
my life has slipped away like this,
and it pisses me off—it's like being
in a movie and everything's in focus
but you. And I haven't been asleep
the whole time either; I think about
the way it goes, all this trouble in the air,
all this bullshit about race, everybody
in the goddamn city half-way scared. I mean

every day I jump out of bed; I look at my
hands, I look at my feet, and I can't remember
growing into them. But tomorrow I was gonna
wake up without my radio, run outdoors and
let the good news graffiti me like
the side wall of a new school in North Philly.
Then I'd drift into the country and spend the day
touching the river—finally learn the word
the water whispers while it works along the shore.
And, for once, by dark I would've been ready
for the sky. I shouldn't worry about that now
though, not with every hard face free
behind the wheel of something fast, not with
all the sidewalks nudging me toward the street.

Earlier this morning I was thinking over
my life, trying to connect all these lines
to the one moment my navel represents,
and a couple days stuck out: that one
Saturday when Dawn hugged me in her basement—
I was only seven and in her ten-year-old arms
my chest felt so full I must've grown
another lung. And this morning I thought I
could explain it perfectly, how if the world
doesn't hold you firmly—and it doesn't—
a hug by a heater in a roachy, dim-lit room
can give you a little traction or something.

But you know that feeling, having a name right
on the tip of your tongue, almost tasting
the letters, then having it slip away,
watching your mind lose its grip and your face
go slack as though somewhere inside yourself
you've just taken one giant step toward dying—
it was like that.

But I don't feel much older
than twenty years ago when my father

blacked my eye 'cause I came home too late
to help carry groceries up from the car. Now
everything hits me like that; the fact
of my being here at all leaves me leaning over
a table, holding my face, but happy
for what might happen next—the possibility
that I could turn a corner and there I'd be
with my life opening like a gallery of beautiful,
beautiful work around me.

I read history and I watch Public TV and I know,
generally speaking, the gentler peoples have been
stomped by the brutes, that if people weren't so good
about cleaning up there could be an ocean as big
as the Atlantic of bright blood and archipelagoes
of bone connecting every continent, but somehow
I always believed my life would break open
the good times—where a woman might close her eyes
and glide behind the lids, where a kid would
catch a caterpillar and just let it go.

But I'm not too worried about it now,
not with the armies filling up the desert, not
now, with the cars here ganging up like
schools of shark at the lights, not with my
last moment buzzing my face like one of those
pesky, drunk, maniacal flies. So, since I'll never
get a chance to love an East Indian lady
tell Debjani, if I had made it past today, I
would have held her like a lantern.

In fact, tell everybody I had this feeling
about the future—I just couldn't get there,
that's all. Tell them there will be cities
where all anyone ever does is rumba and throw
toucans into the air—a couple weeks from now
I bet it's all gonna turn around. I bet

in a little while the constellations
will grow new stars and the wings
of night-flying bugs will pick up the music.